GRACE NOTES
Adjuncts to Worship

by David R. Keeston

ISBN 1 85852 217 X

Text © 2002 by David R. Keeston
Music and Lyrics © 2002 by David R. Keeston and Simon Tatnall

Illustrations © 2002 Francesca Flannery

Printed by Newnorth, Bedford

CONTENTS

BIBLE REFERENCES

Bystanders

The Bread and Wine	Mark 14:22-24
The Bowl and the Towel	John 13:3-9
The Purple Robe	Mark 15:16-20
The Nails	Luke 23:32-33
The Money Bag	Luke 22:1-5
The Crown of Thorns	Matthew 27:27-30
The Shroud	John 20:1-8

Observers

Eutychus	Acts 20:7-12
Priscilla	Acts 18:1-3
Andrew	John 1:35-41
Mary, wife of Clopas	John 19:25
Rachel and Joel	Luke 2:6-7, 15-19

Transfiguration   Matthew 17:1-8

Mordecai's Choice   Book of Esther

INTRODUCTION

This is a collection of sketches, monologues and songs for use in worship on various occasions. The majority of them are not designed to form the centre-piece of an act of worship, but are used to open acts of worship, or to illustrate aspects of the Christian life. All of them were written for specific occasions, but can be used in many different circumstances, though not necessarily at different times of the year.

Any musician will tell you that a grace note is a note added to a melody to make the music sound more decorative. They are usually denoted in smaller notes than the rest of the music, in order not to obscure the main melody and to indicate that they are optional extras, because a musician will also tell you that you can usually omit the grace notes without ruining the piece of music.

Both of those statements are true: but it is also true to say that grace notes can embellish a piece of music, save it from blandness and (if used properly) can lift the spirits of those who hear them. Hence the name of this collection of meditations, worship songs and sketches.

BYSTANDERS

A series of monologues for the Sundays in Lent

A local Methodist church had used a series of Lent readings which involved the placing of symbols at the foot of a (deliberately) roughly-made wooden cross situated at the front of the church. These readings were each used immediately after the first hymn (in place of the opening prayers in a traditional Methodist 'five hymn sandwich' service). The symbols, in order of the Sundays in Lent and Easter were: Bread and Wine, Bowl and Towel, Purple Robe, Nails, Moneybag, Crown of Thorns.

Each week, a reader would come to the front of the church, do a reading, and then place their designated symbol at or on the cross. On Easter Sunday, the cross, which was covered in chicken wire, would be decorated with flowers by the congregation, each person bringing up a spring flower, to represent the Resurrection.

The church in question had used this format for a number of years. They liked the symbols but wanted to change the liturgy, so they asked me to write something different which still used the same symbols. I was happy to do so, but added a symbol – The Shroud – so that there was a reader still on Easter morning.

With the single exception of Mary of Magdala, each character in this set of readings is, strictly speaking, non-existent. They describe characters from the Bible, and though they are not themselves characters from the Bible, people like them must have existed – carpenters, blacksmiths, scribes, soldiers. They have little in common with each other, beyond the fact that they were – even the Temple scribe – ordinary people whose lives were touched in one way or another by the life (and indeed, death) of Jesus of Nazareth.

These pieces are not readings – they must be performed, and I make no apologies for saying that. There are some who would say that 'performance' has no part in worship, that everything done 'before God' must be one hundred percent 'genuine', from the heart, with no element of acting. Usually, it is people who have not had to go into the pulpit Sunday by Sunday, even when one's mother has died, the bills are piling up behind the clock on the mantelpiece, one's spouse has just announced an affair with a colleague at work, and one's teenage child has only that morning denounced Christianity as a sham designed to keep control of society, and then preach on hope in the prophecy of Isaiah. Believe me, there are times when the art of performance comes to the fore for any regular worship leader.

Since these pieces are designed to be performed then, it was tempting to include at the beginning of each piece a little pen portrait of the character of the speaker, in order to give the performer an idea of how it should be performed. In practice, beyond a few indications of vocal mood, I deleted these pen portraits and 'direction'.

Each piece was actually written with a particular performer in mind, and they naturally interpreted them for themselves in much the way I had envisaged them performing the pieces anyway; and experience has shown that most people do the same thing naturally, even if the piece is not written for them specifically. By reading the text several times through, they form in their own minds a picture of the character, and perform the piece in accordance with that mental picture. An attempt at outside direction often ends up confusing the performer and diminishing the performance – it becomes merely a reading.

There is a prayer which linked the pieces together week by week, in addition to the laying of the symbol on the cross, and this is appended at the end of this section.

Do not, under any circumstances, give this to a person 'cold', on the day on which it is to be used in worship and ask them to perform it. Make sure it has been thoroughly rehearsed beforehand, including any movement. **Do,** by all means, allow the performer to change the odd word or phrase they find awkward to say naturally. Although, like every author, I would like to think that these are precisely the right words in the right order, I am not so naïve that I expect every word to be delivered exactly in the order they are written, nor so prissy as to demand that each piece must be performed word for word. The effect, the performance, is what is important, so if a word detracts from the performance, change the word by all means. The only thing I would ask is that you do not change it out of all recognition and still call it mine!

David R. Keeston

THE BREAD AND WINE

My name is Sarah. My husband Ariel owns the inn where Jesus and his friends met for the Passover. It was Ariel who made the wine Jesus poured out and I was the one who made the bread – and, after Ariel had taken the lamb to be sacrificed at the Temple, I dressed it and prepared it, and made all the dishes for the Passover meal.

Apart from the lamb, which is really quite easy to prepare to be honest, everything else – the bitter herbs and the salt water, and the sweet dish, and the hyssop – they all just have to be gathered, and washed, and presented: but the bread and the wine . . . they're different. It's when I'm making bread that I remember Jesus most. It takes so much effort and skill to make good bread. You need strong arms and hard hands to make good bread: to make the dough, and knead it and pound it. My mother Miriam used to say that she always made the best bread, the lightest bread, the most filling bread, when she had 'had words' with my father or one of her friends . . . and I know what she means! It is as though all the frustrations of life, all the disappointments, all the worries that beset you . . . it's as if all of those can be pounded out and poured into that dough.

We don't *think* about bread, do we? It's just there, like wine: just the staple things of life – but it's a miracle, really. I mean, how often do we think about the greatness of the God who could provide us with that delicate kind of grass, which provides those hard little seeds, which can be ground into that life-giving ordinary miraculous stuff we call flour, which makes the bread which we so often take for granted . . . and Ariel says the same about his vineyard. He says that when you pour out wine which is good, which is clear and deep and ruby red, you can almost smell the sunshine and the richness of the earth which were poured into it as the grapes grew pouring out again into your cup . . . another gift of God.

It's no wonder Jesus compared himself to bread and wine, then, is it?

I remember he had this incredible gift: he could listen to you, pouring out your story like wine into a goblet, letting go of your worries like you were talking to the dough you were pounding on the table, and he could  make you feel that, at that moment, and just for that minute, you were the most important person in the world. It was almost as if he could let himself be pounded like that bread. It was almost as if, like the bread, he could give you the strength to go on . . . and then for a while you would feel better . . . it was almost as if he could let himself be poured out like that wine, and listening to him was like having sunshine, like having life itself, poured out all over you.

So I remember Jesus. I don't remember him as being overbearing, or self-important, or harsh, like you'd expect someone to be who had that much power. I remember how he served us all in ordinary things, and loved us all, and made us feel that, just for once, we were important to God.

I don't remember him when people talk about that day he rode into Jerusalem, or the day he cleared the Temple.

I remember him whenever I make the bread and pour the wine.

THE BOWL AND TOWEL

My wife, Sarah, is always particularly careful about getting ready for Passover. You know what women can be like: they always like to think *they* are in charge, and sometimes it's better to let them think so! Anyway, Sarah would always spend a couple of days beforehand asking all the obvious questions – had I done this, had I done that, and 'Ariel, have you made arrangements for the sacrifice? Are we sharing the lamb with Reuben's family again this year?'

She could drive you mad, my Sarah – but at least everything got done. So I was a bit surprised when someone called down from the Upper Room. I was even more surprised when I realised it was him – Jesus, you know – although perhaps I shouldn't have been.

He wanted a bowl of water and a towel. I was a bit nonplussed, actually. Usually, everything you might need for Passover was ready – Sarah saw to that. I wondered what sort of bowl I should give him. It didn't seem right to give him the ordinary, workday earthenware I had in the inn. I had three. They were all plain clay – undecorated, chipped, stained. They were used for everything. I used them for washing down the tables. Travellers used them to wash their feet sometimes . . . and as for a towel! All I had were the rags cut from the cloth we couldn't use anymore for anything else . . . we're a plain, poor family, really. Everything gets twice as much use as it is designed for. The bowl and towel didn't seem good enough for someone who had been hailed as a king only the week before.

Anyway, it didn't matter. Jesus just smiled and said, 'That bowl will do, Ariel!' and grabbed the one I was about to use to swill down the floor, and the clean towel – well, alright then, bit of rag – I'd just slung over my shoulder.

I know I probably shouldn't have done, but I followed him back to the room his disciples were in. I wanted to see what he was going to do with them. I dithered a bit outside the room, and by the time I got brave enough to slip through the door, Jesus was kneeling at the feet of one of his disciples – it was Simon bar Jonah the fisherman, I think – and was actually washing his feet! There'd obviously been a bit of a fuss about it. Simon was looking a bit uncomfortable. No wonder really. I mean, it's a servant's job, washing people's feet, isn't it? You wouldn't expect the Messiah, the Son of God, to be washing *your* feet: much more likely that you would be washing his!

He did a proper job, though – it wasn't just a sprinkle and a quick wipe for show. He really put his all into that feet washing. He made even that menial job seem really important: he knelt like a servant and gave that menial task a kind of royal dignity.

He took the most ordinary of objects – just a chipped bowl and an old towel – and used them to make us feel like we had witnessed God himself at work. And although what he did was the picture of humility, it was us who felt humbled by his simple goodness.

THE PURPLE ROBE

It was good wool, that's what really upset me to begin with: and it was a good twill piece, by the time I had finished carding and spinning and weaving it . . .

Everyone agrees my mother was the best spinner and weaver in our village, and when we moved into Jerusalem, I could hold my own with the best cloth workers in the street, given good wool. And it *was* good wool, so I had lavished on that weave every skill and art my mother taught me . . . and my husband lost it! He lost it!

I rue the day I ever let Benjamin persuade me to get it dyed – and royal purple! It was a mistake, really, but Benjamin was so pleased with the way it had turned out, and he always had an eye on the main chance. As a minor scribe in the Temple, he thought that we could present the robe to Caiaphas – or even Herod Antipas the King – and earn some kudos.

I couldn't believe it when he sneaked into the house that day. I had sent him to Jethro the dyer to collect the robe and he crawls into the house like a whipped cur, empty-handed and trying to pretend nothing had happened. Really, sometimes he must think I came up the Jordan on a camel!

'Where is it?' I ask him.

He mumbles something, I tell him to speak up, and then he tells me. He's lost it, he tries to explain. He tries to sell me some complete load of nonsense about Roman auxiliaries stopping him in the street and demanding the robe. They were drunk, apparently – no change there, then – and kept roaring with laughter and saying it was for a king.

'Didn't you stand up to them?' I asked Benjamin. Well, of course he didn't. He's a scribe, a priest. He isn't going to stand up to a bunch of drunken Roman soldiers, is he? Not if he values his life, he isn't . . .

Benjamin told me that they disappeared into the Antonia Palace after they stole the robe. I was so blazing angry that I was out of the door before Benjamin could stop me. No Roman soldier was going to steal *my* work and get away with it. Robe for a king, indeed . . . well, maybe it was, but *I* was the one to decide which king to give it to, and they were going to give it back or feel the rough edge of my tongue. Probably both, if I'm honest . . .

So I burst into the courtyard, looking around quickly for the likely candidates – and then I saw who they had put the robe on, and my words dried in my mouth and my anger evaporated. In its place all I could feel was the most tremendous sorrow.

I truly wished I had never thought to make that robe. It was my Jesus, you see: it was my Jesus they had put my robe on, my robe I'd been so proud of. My Jesus, who made nearly everyone think they were special to him, who had really bought Torah alive for me for the first time, who had preached, and healed, and offered hope, and shown us God. They had tortured him and they had sullied all my work by their cruelty, but that wasn't what was really important. It was far worse than that.

They had beaten him, you see. And whipped him. And twisted briars together to make a kind of perversion of a Roman victor's laurel wreath . . . and then they had put my robe on him, *(bitterly)* a real finishing touch, that.

The odd thing was, for all that he could barely stand, and was sweating in agony, and had his eyes half-closed by beatings, and was bleeding from many places – *(softly)* oh, so many places – he looked far more noble, and kingly, and even serene, than any ordinary man had the right to look after that sort of treatment.

Then, just as I was turning away, he opened his eyes, and caught sight of me. I could almost swear that he nearly smiled. I'm certain he went to raise his hand in a kind of blessing . . . the soldier nearest him hit his arm with a staff, but nonetheless I *knew* . . . so I turned and went home.

Benjamin asked me about the robe. I told him not to worry. I told him it had been delivered to the king. And then I went into the sleeping room in the dark depths at the back of the house and I lay down in the dark for a long time. And I wept for a king.

THE NAILS

Most men in this city learnt their trade from their father and I'm no different. My father used to tell me that *his* father told him that one of our ancestors worked on the rebuilding of the Temple. Not *this* Temple, you understand – not Herod's temple. No no, he meant the one they restored after the return from Exile in Babylon! Well, it might be true, I suppose. I'm not really all that bothered. I don't have much time for all those airy-fairy stories. I suppose it's because I like to *see* what I'm working with. I like the certainty of what I do.

I know that if I get some good quality iron – or brass, or whatever metal or alloy I'm working with at the time – and I heat it in just the way my father taught me, for just the right amount of time, then I can beat it and bend it into exact shapes. I like the certainty of my craft, the deftness, the skill and the speed you need to pull the metal from the forge at just the right moment. If you pull it too soon, you see, it's not malleable enough. It's difficult to strike right, and it shatters.

If you leave it in the forge too long, it's almost like quicksilver and you cannot work it at all. But do it right, just right and you can make just about anything. I mostly make big things – gates and hinges, and wheel rims. Things like that. When I'm at a bit of a loose end, I take the leavings and make smaller, useful things that are quick and easy.

Mostly I make nails.

Although I can make all sorts of nails – brass nails, for example: delicate little things for attaching *mezuzim* to doorposts – nearly all the nails I make are big, clumsy looking things made of iron and tempered so that they can be driven hard through one or two layers of wood. Useful things, nails, though they're all much of a muchness, really. Sharpened, tempered slivers of metal. Workaday. Useful. Ten a penny . . .

I suppose smithying looks dramatic to the outsider. Hot flames, hot metal. The clanging of hammers, the swift movements. We get loads of people who stop and watch us working. We're used to it. I tend to ignore the gawpers, or I tell them to get lost and don't stand in my light – all except once, one day.

I was working in the heat of my forge, starting the fire, when suddenly the light from the entrance dimmed a little. I looked up and there stood that preacher everyone had been talking about. Jesus of Nazareth. He smiled and asked my name. When I told him, he smiled again and reached out his hand to clasp my upper arm and said, 'Pleased to meet you, Moishe. I'm Jesus.'

I am not very religious and I would have just dismissed him, to be honest, if I hadn't felt that hand on the bare skin of my arm. It was rough. The palm and fingers were calloused . . . He had workman's hands, this Jesus. Someone told me later he had been a carpenter and a good one. I listened to him because of those hands. I don't have a lot of time for the soft-handed priests and scribes. No – more than that. I don't have *any* time for them. What do they know about hard work? But because of those callouses, because of those hands, I sat and talked with Jesus while I waited for the fire to get hot enough: and he changed my life in about five minutes. I finally realised that God isn't just for the soft hands of this world, but for everyone: *(holds up hands)* that God made these and put the skill in them and rejoices in my work as much as he rejoices in the worship of the pious, if we do what we do for him. Jesus taught me that even the iron we rip from the earth is God's gift . . . he was a great guy, that calloused-handed Carpenter.

I sat by my forge a long time the day they crucified him. It didn't take me long to realise, you see, that some of the huge clumsy nails I made the day he talked to me were almost certainly the ones that they used to nail him to the cross. Someone corrupted the gift God gave me, to forge and work good tools, good nails, to pierce the calloused hands which changed the life of the smith who made them.

Tragic, really. Even – dare I say it – ironic?

THE MONEY BAG

Caiaphas sent a servant to me, with a message to bring some Temple coinage to him. He wanted thirty silver pieces and he wanted them straight away.

It was an unusual request, but I had worked with Caiaphas long enough to know that he did nothing without purpose. A cold, calculating man, Caiaphas. So I counted out the money and looked around for something to put it in – it isn't easy to carry thirty silver pieces, even with both hands: they weren't little, those Temple coins.

I was looking for a piece of linen to wrap them in, but in the very male environment of the Temple, could I find a piece? Of course not! In the end, I had no choice but to use my own purse. I was very reluctant, I have to say. It may only have been a little leather drawstring bag to anyone else, but it had importance to me: my mother had bought it from a Syrian trader in Damascus when we were visiting family up there. She had presented it to me, filled with half a talent of gold, when I set out for Jerusalem to sit at the feet of Gamaliel and become a scribe.

'There you are, Simeon, my son!' she had said. 'A present for you! Give the gold to Gamaliel – but it carries in it my love for you as well!'

I never saw her again. She died from a fever whilst I was on my way to Jerusalem. By the time I got the news she had been buried three days. Of course, I gave the gold to Gamaliel – but I kept the bag. Call me sentimental, if you like, but I kept that little bag tied to my belt the whole time I sat at Gamaliel's feet. It was empty, but full of love.

When I got the request from Caiaphas, I was a bit older and a bit more circumspect. Working with Temple figures and Temple money tends to make you suspicious of everybody, I guess. I had no idea what Caiaphas needed thirty shekels for at the end of the day, but I took them along anyway. He was closeted with an intense looking young man, dressed in rough travelling clothes. He looked like a Zealot to me – maybe even one of those knife-wielding *sicarii*. He was still gesturing towards Caiaphas very aggressively when I entered, but all I heard him say was ' . . . and I say it *will* happen' before Caiaphas silenced him with a gesture.

'Simeon,' said the High Priest, 'this is Judas Iscariot. He is a disciple of Jesus, the Nazarene. He wants to persuade me that this Jesus is indeed the Messiah for whom we all so devoutly wait. If Judas is right, then he should give up Jesus to the authorities – to me. We will listen to what he has to say and form our own opinion. If indeed he is the Messiah, surely God will give us some sign. If not . . . well, we can deal with him. I wonder what Simeon thinks of this Jesus – give us the benefit of your opinion, Simeon.'

I knew then I was in danger. Caiaphas never asked for your opinion unless he wanted to trip you up. The trouble was, Caiaphas had obviously heard that I had been amongst those listening to Jesus' teaching and preaching in Jerusalem and the surrounding villages. Any opinion I gave was going to be the wrong one.

Caiaphas saw my hesitation and smiled. It was the smile of a wolf. He spoke to Judas again. 'The trouble is, Judas,' he said, 'Jesus is so elusive. We need you to tell us where he is going to be tomorrow night. You need to guarantee that information, and if you do, I shall act – and then we will see which of us is right: you, or me.'

Judas looked at me: I knew he recognised me. He had seen me talking to Jesus on many occasions. He had even eaten at my table with Jesus. He knew that I, too, in my own way, was a disciple. I was convinced that Jesus was the Messiah and I knew that Judas was too: the only difference between us was that Judas had courage and I was a coward. I could tell by the way Caiaphas spoke which way the wind was blowing. Jesus, I was sure, was about to be disposed of – but I cannot rid myself of the feeling that, if I had only spoken out then, when Caiaphas asked my opinion, I might have been able to do something, to say something, to prevent what happened next.

'Simeon,' said Caiaphas smoothly and softly, 'what do *you* think of this Jesus?'

It seemed like a long time passed before I heard a strange voice, which turned out to be mine, saying, 'I do not know him, sir. I can have no opinion.'

Both Judas and Caiaphas turned their stare on me – one cold and calculating, the other hot and outraged. I think I nearly fainted under the intensity of their stares. Finally, Caiaphas said, 'Very well, Simeon. Give Judas the money and then go back to your duties.'

I held out the bag to Judas – the bag which had once been filled with my mother's love and now was filled with the cost of cowardice. Judas wouldn't take it at first, but Caiaphas insisted. The blood money had to be taken, he said, as a sign of good faith. Judas finally snatched it from my hand and I left.

They say that Judas betrayed Jesus and that's why he killed himself. It might be true – but the cynic I have become often wonders whether Judas' death wasn't the result of one of Caiaphas' 'tidying up' operations. Whatever happened, I have to live with the knowledge that Judas didn't betray Jesus on his own: we all did it. And every one of us who betrayed Jesus then betrays him again when we don't stand up at the right moment and speak out against the Caiaphases of this world.

You haven't told me your name . . . my name *is* Simeon – but it might as well be Judas.

THE CROWN OF THORNS

I really love dates, don't you? To be honest, there isn't much I *do* like about this benighted province. I'm no politician, but I really do not understand why we're here at all. I'm a Gaul; I'm used to the cool north, not this fly-ridden dusty heat. The people are surly and there's always the threat of rebellion. I'm supposed to be a proud soldier of Rome, but every time I walk down the street, I get stared at or ignored and I can never decide which is worse. They either ignore you, treat you as if you're not there, a non-person, or they stare at you as if you're some lump of camel dung they've just scraped off their sandal.

That's why I love dates. After all the stew and the heat of Jerusalem, standing guard at the gates of the Palace in the heat of the day, it's just bliss to bite into one. I can never work out how it is that a date can be standing in the heat of the sun all day and yet be so cool on the tongue when you bite into it. Gifts from the gods, dates, no doubt about that, and I was just biting into one and feeling its juice cool on my tongue, when I turned into the courtyard.

I've served with Legio X Fretensis, but I'm in charge of a section of Syrian auxiliaries now: they like to think of themselves as Roman, but they aren't real soldiers, these Syrians. I reckon they'd run away if they got into a real fight. They're basically scum, like soldiers everywhere, but they're undisciplined scum. Bullies, to be honest.

I had to go and check on a guard placement in the city and I left them in charge of a prisoner in the courtyard, one waiting to go back before the governor. The governor had ordered the prisoner flogged, so I left them to that routine task. When I came back into the courtyard, I could hear them taunting the prisoner and I could hear the thump of fists hitting the prisoner's ribcage.

Typical, I thought. Typical of the Syrians to go over the top.

They'd blindfolded him and put a purple robe on him – although Jupiter knows where they got that from – and had flogged him till the bloody skin hung off his back in shreds. Just as I opened my mouth to speak, I heard Fretellus shout – it would be him – 'Who hit you then, prophet? If you're a real prophet, surely you can tell?'

The thing that really got me, though, was the crown they'd made. Typical of these Middle Eastern types, they'd tried to make him something which looked like the sunburst crowns of their supposedly

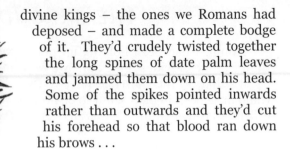

divine kings – the ones we Romans had deposed – and made a complete bodge of it. They'd crudely twisted together the long spines of date palm leaves and jammed them down on his head. Some of the spikes pointed inwards rather than outwards and they'd cut his forehead so that blood ran down his brows . . .

I've seen lots of executions. I've used a *flagellum* myself to flog prisoners. I'm an old hand . . . but I'd never seen anything like this. The prisoner – Yeshua was his name, but we called him Jesus – stood and took all that pain, all that suffering and rather than become humiliated, seem to rise above it all somehow – like he was in the divine realm already. He looked at those auxiliaries with *compassion*, almost pity, and didn't say a word. Then he turned and looked at me as I crossed the courtyard, ready to lead him back to Pilate.

I'm a soldier. Put a sword in one hand and a shield in the other and I let them do the talking, but I'm no good with words, so I can't properly describe how he looked at me. But there he was, covered in blood and dust, sweating, obviously in agony and with blood running down his face from the spikes of the date palms, whose fruit I had just used to refresh my mouth, whose juice I could still taste . . . and he looked like a king.

I don't know much about this crazy Jewish religion, with its single god – unnatural, I call it, to have only one god – but I'd heard how some people had said this dusty preacher from the north was supposed to be the king they'd all been waiting for.

Well, I'm here to tell you that he looked like one. When I looked into his eyes, it was if I looked into heaven itself. My men had flogged him, stripped him and cut his head with the leaves of something which provided such sweetness . . . but he wasn't defeated by what we'd done to him. I expected to see rage, but I saw pity. I expected to see defiance, but I saw compassion. I expected to see hatred, but I saw understanding.

Mind you, I've never eaten a date since: for some reason, they always taste bitter in my mouth now.

THE SHROUD

I think I had been holding up pretty well, really. After all the trauma of the previous three days, we were all in a daze. Seeing Jesus die like that, in that horrible way, you would have thought that we would have been in pieces, but to be honest we were so stunned it was difficult to feel anything. It was all over, and we couldn't take it in.

One of our people had gone to Pilate and begged to be allowed to take Jesus' body down from the cross before Passover came in. It was a brave thing to do and we were very grateful to Joseph, but by the time he got permission all we had time to do was wrap the body in a shroud and put him in Joseph's tomb – the one he had prepared for himself, I mean. Then we had to leave him there.

I know it sounds stupid, but I wasn't ready for that – just leaving him there, I mean. I hadn't been allowed to actually handle the body myself and I couldn't get used to the idea that he was dead: I couldn't relate the coldness of death with the warm, vital, bursting-with-life person I knew Jesus to be. So when they rolled that stone across the  entrance of the tomb, I couldn't get rid of the feeling that we were deserting him. The thought that we were just abandoning him to the darkness of the tomb and the cold of the night was overwhelming. I wanted to get him a blanket, or something.

I felt there ought to be something we could still do for him . . . it was his mother, Mary, who asked me if I would come back with her to the tomb once Passover was ended, to prepare the body for burial properly. The thought that we could do that last thing for him was all that kept me going over the next couple of days. Without the thought that there was that one way left to honour him, I think I would have collapsed there and then . . .

As it was, I couldn't wait for Jesus' mother and the rest of them. I decided to wait at the tomb until they arrived, so I got up early and went. I don't know what I thought I could do on my own, really; that stone took three men to put it in place so I wasn't going to be able to shift it, but there you go – what law says you have to be thinking straight two days after you've seen your best friend executed? I don't know one, but no doubt some dried up old Pharisee somewhere will come up with an obscure verse from Leviticus to cover it . . .

It was very early, but already you could sense that it was going to be a beautiful day. There was that hush you get at dawn, just before the sun leaps over the hills, but when I saw that gaping black hole where the stone should be, I knew something terrible had happened. I have to be honest and say that in some ways I was relieved when I realised the body was gone. You might wonder why. You see, I wouldn't have put it past some of Jesus' enemies to have desecrated his body in some way – so its disappearance was less of a shock than it might have been.

All I could think of, though, was to get to Simon Peter and the others and tell them what had happened, though I don't know *what* I thought *he* could do about it. At that time in his life he wasn't a great one in a crisis, wasn't Simon. Liable to rush round in circles and lash out in all directions, if you follow me. Ask Malchus, the High Priest's servant, if you don't believe me.

Anyway, as soon as I told them the body was missing, off go Simon Peter and John like they've got a whole Roman Legion on their tails, to check – typical men, they were, they wouldn't believe a woman until they had seen it with their own eyes.

I had already run the whole distance, so I had no chance of keeping up with them. By the time I got back to the tomb, they'd already been inside it. Simon Peter and John were sitting on the ground outside, staring at the grave cloth we'd wrapped Jesus in. I'd never seen Peter look so desolate, not ever, not even when he crept back into the house in the early hours of Friday morning, after they'd arrested Jesus. They just said, 'He's gone, Mary', and wandered off out of the garden, almost dazed.

It's funny, really, because it was when Simon said those words – 'He's gone, Mary' – that it really hit me, all that had happened over the last few days, and I knew that he really *had* gone, and it was us, we disciples, we human beings, who had failed him. We couldn't even bury him properly. We couldn't even get his funeral right. It was the last straw. It was all too much, and it just broke me up. I just stood there, unable to move, and I cried.

Actually, I didn't just cry – I *howled*. It was like it all welled out all at once, everything that had happened over the previous few days. I couldn't have stopped for anybody . . . but eventually, I heard a voice in front of me. Even as I cried, I thought, 'That's funny, I didn't hear them come.'

There were two men and I think they were dressed in white, but to be honest I couldn't have said for sure, my eyes were that full of tears. They asked me why I was crying . . . well, I ask you, a woman standing outside a new tomb, crying – what did they think I was crying for?

Anyway, I told them.

Before the two in front of me could answer, I heard another voice behind me. I thought he was the gardener. I was still weeping, you see, and still half-blinded with tears, and when he asked the same question I turned and held out the shroud to him and I begged him. I begged him to tell me where Jesus was, if he knew, if it was him who had taken the body away. By that stage, all my pride was gone. I would have begged the Procurator himself to tell me, if I thought he knew.

He didn't answer, although in a way he did. He said my name. Just the once, and quietly, he said my name . . . and I knew it was him . . . it was *him* . . . Jesus . . . and he said my name . . . 'Mary'.

You know how the morning starts? You know how, even though it's still dark, there's a moment when the whole world seems to hold its breath and then there's a pause as the dawn grows and then the birds start to sing – just a few at first and then they all join in, and then everything seems to change in an instant, from deep darkness to amazing light?

Well, *that's* how it was: just like that. From darkest night to the most incredible dawn . . . and suddenly I was babbling and Jesus was talking and giving me a message for the others like he always did and I was still crying, and then I was running, and even as I ran, still with the shroud in my hand, I was still crying, but this time because there was no other way to express my joy.

Just for a moment, I wondered whether the others would believe me, but not for long. Inside my head, I could still hear his voice saying my name . . . 'Mary'. And in a funny sort of way, I didn't care whether they believed me or not, because he had changed my world in an instant, with one word, and I *knew*. I *knew,* as I know now, that Jesus lives.

And I danced as I ran.

THE PRAYER

(said after each presentation)

Will you pray with me?

Father God,

you made so many marvellous things

when you made the world and its people:

but help us to remember you

and the love you showed us in Jesus,

not just in the things which make us stop

and praise your name,

but also in the ordinary things of life

which we take for granted

but are just as much your gift.

Amen.

A HYMN FOR GOOD FRIDAY

We took the Word eternal,
Through whom we came to be,
And stretched the hands that made us
To nail them to a tree:
We took the love he offered
and spat it in his face
And stripped the King of glory
Of everything but grace.

Oh, Jesus, son of Heaven,
What makes me worth the Cross?
When all my deeds deny you,
Can I be such a loss?
Oh, loving Lord and master,
Why should you die for me?
My sin has crucified you,
And yet you set me free.

Oh, gentle son of Mary,
Who taught us how to live,
Such pain cries out for justice,
And yet you cry, 'Forgive!'
Your cross stands stark and brutal,
You bear the cruellest scorn:
For darkness is the herald
of God's redeeming dawn.

Can be sung to tunes of the same metre as 'O sacred head, sore wounded'

Good Friday Hymn

Legato

We took the word e - ter - nal, through whom we came to be, and stretched the hands that made us to nail them to a tree: We took the love he

Oh, Jesus, son of Heaven,
What makes me worth the Cross?
When all my deeds deny you,
Can I be such a loss?
Oh, loving Lord and master,
Why should you die for me?
My sin has crucified you,
And yet you set me free.

Oh, gentle son of Mary,
Who taught us how to live,
Such pain cries out for justice,
And yet you cry, 'Forgive!'
Your cross stands stark and brutal,
You bear the cruellest scorn:
For darkness is the herald
of God's redeeming dawn.

CROSS-ROADS
A Good Friday play for five voices

At about the same time as the Lent 'meditation' series was written, an ecumenical Open Air Service was being planned for the end of a Good Friday Walk of Witness.

The site chosen for the service was outside one of the participating churches in the local pedestrianised High Street, where two roads crossed. Again, I have not included any detailed stage directions in this piece, since whoever performs it is likely to do so in radically different conditions to those in which it was originally performed; however, simplicity is the key to the staging of this piece. It is actually capable of being performed anywhere.

Angelo	So, who wants to start? Who's going to begin to tell us what happened here?
Jo	Maggie, Mags! You tell him.
Maggie	Me? Why me?
Jo	You were there right from the start. If anyone should know what's going on, you should.
Simon	I was there right from the start, too.
Jo	Yeah, but you never got close to him like Maggie. She really was there from the very beginning. Got close.
Tony	*(sneers)* Very close indeed, I heard.
Maggie	*(angrily)* That's a lie, Tony! You people!
Tony	What people? We Romans, you mean?
Maggie	No! You men! Roman, Greek, Jew – you all think with the same organ –
Jo	– shame it's not the brain!

They come closer together, squaring up to each other

Angelo	Woah, woah, children – please! Let's settle down here. There's no need for any of this!
Simon	You want to hear the story, don't you . . . whoever you are. I don't know your name. Who are you, anyway?
Maggie	He's some kind of Roman, isn't he? *(turns to Angelo)* Aren't you?
Angelo	No, I'm –
Tony	He's not one of us! He wasn't there when it happened – and anyway, he doesn't even look Roman: looks more like one of you kikes.
Simon	Greaseball!
Tony	Yid!
Simon	Garlic breath!
Tony	Hook nose!
Simon	Barbarian!
Tony	Coward!
Tony **Simon**	*(shout) Murderer!*
Angelo	*(shouts)* Enough!

Pause

Angelo	So tell us your story, Maggie. Why are you here?
Maggie	Must I?
Angelo	You want people to understand, don't you? You don't want the story to die?
Jo	The story won't die, whatever happens.
Maggie	It's not a story! It's not just some glossy book you can pick up and put down at will!
Simon	You can't skip over the nasty bits.
Maggie	No! You've got to live them – and live with them.

Angelo	So tell us *your* story.
Maggie	I was born in Magadala – that's why Jo calls me 'Maggie', but really my name is Mary. My father wasn't particularly well off and neither was he particularly religious. He wasn't all that clever, either – he thought Greek culture was something you found in a pot of yoghurt! Didn't stop him trying to copy them, though . . . he married me off to a merchant from Damascus.
Angelo	Was it a good marriage?
Maggie	Are you joking? I was a chattel – just a *something* to him, not a *someone*. We never had children and although I was sad about it for a while, I looked upon barrenness as God's blessing after a while, because it wasn't long before he had another woman on his arm, then another, then another, as he got bored with them and me. He ended up loaning me out to his friends.
Tony	He did *what?*
Maggie	He loaned me out to his friends. Traded me for favours. I told you – he was a merchant. I was just another commodity to him. Eventually, he died. His family said it was dropsy. I think it was the pox. He left me with nothing but a house, a wardrobe full of fancy clothes and a pile of debts. So I sold the house, paid off the debts and moved back to Magdala with the wardrobe; then I sold the only thing I had to sell – my body.
Simon	How could you do that?
Maggie	*(laughs bitterly)* Easily. It meant nothing to me; by then I hated men almost as much as I hated myself. I was worthless, useless, scum.
Tony	So what changed things for you?
Maggie	Jesus changed things – Jesus, the man you Romans are crucifying today.
Tony	I'm not.

Maggie	*(fiercely)* Don't shirk responsibility for what you are doing!
Tony	I'm not proud of what I've done!
Maggie	Neither was I. Proud of myself, I mean. I was on the point of ending it all when I heard that Jesus was in the town I was staying in. I went to hear him speak: he changed my life.
Simon	But what did he say?
Maggie	I can't tell you what he said – it would take too long. All I can say is that what he taught that day made me realise that everything I had ever done – unspeakable things, vile things – was wiped out in God's forgiveness. He made me feel what I hadn't felt since my mother died: he made me feel valued. He made me realise that, no matter what everybody else called me – tart, slapper, prossie – God loved the person under the paint. I followed him from then on, and he's brought me here. So *you (pointing at Tony)* could murder him!

Angelo	What about you, Simon?
Simon	*(aggressively)* What *about* me?
Angelo	Why are you here?
Simon	Why ask me – why not ask those gawpers out there? *(points to crowd)* Why not ask them why they are here?
Angelo	Well –
Simon	No, don't bother, I'll do it!
Angelo	Don't worry about them. Just tell us your story. What road brought you here?
Simon	But it's people like that who have got to hear! They mill around the market, pick things up, barter, haggle, maybe buy a few things, and here we are, oppressed and conquered by gentile scum like him – *(points to Tony)* and these people just accept it – get

on with their lives as if nothing has happened. Look at them! Gawpers! Staring at us like we were slaves being sold in the market! Half dead! Not even knowing they're alive! They need to wake up!

Jo Why are you so angry?

Simon Why? Because we are God's people, a chosen people in a holy land and we behave as if we don't care. We see the Law violated every day, people treated like slaves and servants by Romans – and we collude with it!

Jo There sometimes have to be – accommodations. Compromises. For the good of the many.

Simon Well, you'd know, wouldn't you – married to Herod's steward!

Tony So why follow Jesus?

Simon Because he's the Messiah! Because I have been fighting all my adult life to be free of you people, so we could *all* be free of you people. I'm a Zealot and I've been waiting for the Messiah and I knew he would come.

Tony But why Jesus? He's no hot-headed Zealot, is he?

Simon You weren't here when he turned over the moneychangers' tables, then? If you'd seen that, you would know he could get angry – and with all the legions of heaven on his side . . .

Maggie If he was going to bring the legions of heaven down on the Romans, Simon, why is he hanging on a cross today?

Simon I don't know! I wish I did . . . Oh, God, yes I do . . . it's because of what he's been telling us all along. He uses the power of love, not hate . . . and you know what Maggie said about feeling worthless? Well, I never felt like that, until I met Jesus. I was totally sure of what I believed and why. My entire life was centred around driving the Romans into the sea. 'God's land for God's people', all that sort of thing. Then I got curious about this Jesus everybody talked

	about . . . so I went to find him. When I first saw him, he was surrounded by people. I'd just got up to him, when he stopped and reached out to a man sitting by the roadside. A blind man. He healed him.
Tony	How?
Simon	Not with grand gestures, not with fine words. He just said, 'Do you want to see?' and touched the bloke's eyes, and you could see the light come back into them . . . it was amazing.
Jo	Why did that make you follow him?
Simon	Because I spent all my time talking about oppression, and injustice, and freedom, and I hadn't even seen the blind man – I hadn't even noticed him by the roadside. You see beggars every day. Jesus saw him and touched him, and healed him – someone of no account, who most of us didn't even acknowledge. He made me look deeper into things, deeper into my own life. He made me begin to look at things in a different way . . . made me see that justice and truth and love are not just *words*, not just empty gestures – they can only be made real in our dealings with each other as individuals. For him, everyone counts – but look, now. Who's going to heal *him*, hanging there, if he won't do it for himself?
Angelo	Do you doubt his power?
Simon	I don't doubt his power to love, mate. Not at all. He changed my life totally – made me see that all my politics, all my grand gestures, all my fierce pride, were worth nothing if I couldn't even see the needs of people I passed in the street every day without a thought. But look at these people passing us by now, staring. Why can't they see that? What is it about us human beings that makes us turn away from life itself?

Angelo	Jo – Joanna?
Jo	Yes? I suppose you're wondering why I am here, aren't you?
Tony	It's a bit odd, love. You're . . . well . . .
Jo	What? Rich? Female?
Tony	No, it's not that. It's that you're almost like one of us.
Jo	Hellenistic, you mean – Greek?
Tony	I suppose.
Jo	Yeah, OK, I'm rich. My husband serves Herod. We've taken on board some of the culture and learning of the Greeks. It doesn't make me less Jewish. Just because I'm a woman, it doesn't make me less human, either.
Tony	Yeah, but this Jesus – he was supposed to be all in favour of the poor, wasn't he?
Jo	Oh, he was all in favour of the poor alright – but he wasn't all in favour of poverty.
Angelo	But haven't you got everything you want in your life? What made you walk this road?
Jo	Everything? Sure, I've got everything. Servants, two different houses – one here in Jerusalem and another in Tiberius – I've been blessed with children and a husband who loves me (and even secretly supports what I am doing). I've got everything – and nothing. You asked me why I followed Jesus – why I and others made his meals, supported him and his disciples financially when necessary, looked after them when they would let us? Because he told the bride-price story – that's why I follow him.
Simon	Bride-price story? I don't understand.
Jo	No, you wouldn't. You probably only listened to the stories of kings and shepherds and farmers and farmers' sons – men's stories! But he told a story just for the women, once. I knew then he understood.

Angelo	What's the story?
Jo	Oh, it's simple. It was about a woman who had one hundred gold coins and one day lost one. She swept the entire house out, took lamps into the dark corners, looked everywhere until she found it. Jesus used it as an example of how much they will rejoice in heaven over even one person who has turned away from God but turns back to God again: but it meant more than that to me.
Tony	What's that got to do with women, particularly? Or brides?
Jo	You've just made my point for me. *You* don't understand, do you?
Tony	Understand *what*? Stop being so obscure!
Jo	Where did the coin come from? I'll tell you. It was sewn to the fringe of her headdress. It was her dowry. It was the only riches she had that could not be taken from her – all she could take away from the marriage if the marriage failed, if her husband divorced her. No wonder she panicked! That one gold coin was a precious part of *all she had*!
Angelo	So what did that make you realise, Jo?
Jo	It made me realise that I lived surrounded by riches and gold – but that none of it was mine. I lived in a golden cage. I thought I was valuable for what I owned, for the servants I could command, or the perfumes, oils and spices I could buy, but I was wrong. If all that disappeared, what was I left with?
Tony	Your bride-price?
Jo	If you like. What I *ought* to be left with is my birthright, granted by God.
Tony	Being Jewish, you mean?
Jo	No! Being *human,* you fool! The gift God gives us all – life itself! My dowry which, like that woman, I so nearly lost. It was that story which convinced me that Jesus understood where I and so many women in our society are – where so many *people* are! I

could see then that Jesus understood that: understood something which I had lost sight of. God values people for who they are, not for their gender, or wealth, or position in society. He doesn't condemn people for their wealth, or their poverty, or their gender, but we condemn ourselves if we allow ourselves to be imprisoned by any of these things – if we allow ourselves to be defined by them. There is no special virtue in poverty or riches, masculinity or femininity. What God asks us to value is our common humanity – and it's a gift we all have.

Angelo   So that's why you follow him?

Jo   Yes. He gave me back the gift of myself, which I so nearly lost in the dazzle of wealth. He unlocked the door which let me out of my cage.

Angelo   So what about you, Tony? Antoninus, the Roman Centurion? Why are you still here? Surely your job is already done? See – Jesus hangs from the cross you put him on!

Tony   Look, I'm a soldier. You can't expect me to be able to bandy words with you people.

Simon   We *Jews*, you mean?

Tony   No, not especially you Jews. Anyone.

Angelo   So don't bandy words. Just tell us your story. Why are you here?

Tony   I suppose I'm here as much because of what Jesus *didn't* do as for what he *did* do.

Angelo   I don't follow you.

Tony   Look, just how many crucifixions have you seen? Actually seen? Ten? Twenty?

Simon   You crucified four hundred of my people at once not so long ago!

Tony   *(quietly)* Yeah – but were *you* there, Simon?

Simon	I saw their corpses hanging –
Tony	*(fiercely)* Yeah, yeah – but did you see 'em die? Were you there when the nails were driven home, when the crosses shuddered down into the sockets we dug for them from the dry earth, were you there to hear the screams?
Simon	No.
Tony	Thought not. Well, I *was* there, see. I *was*.
Angelo	It affected you badly, then?
Tony	To be honest, no. Have you any idea how many people I have nailed to a cross? Have you? Well, it's hundreds for sure. Might even be a thousand. After a while they all merge into one. It becomes *routine*, God forgive me! *(speaks as in military manual)* Lay the cross down, lay the prisoner on it –
Jo	*(covers her ears)* Oh stop, please, stop! I can't bear it!
Tony	– pinion arms and legs, position nails on wrists – on *wrists*, mark you, not palms, otherwise the weight of the prisoner tears the nails through his hands (and ankles, not feet, for the same reason) and then make sure the first few blows are sharp and heavy. Lift cross, place in socket, drop. Routine.
Angelo	So what was different this time?
Tony	I don't remember the faces, or the names, or ages, or the crimes of any of the people I've put to death. Not one of them – it's easier that way. Insulates you a bit. The thing is, one way or the other, they nearly always curse you.
Angelo	When you crucify them?
Tony	Yeah. See, they're all different and all much the same. You see the same expressions of shock, and outrage, and fear – and even sometimes pride. Some struggle all the way to the place of execution. Some go quietly, almost in shock. Some can't stop talking, keep begging for mercy – and some walk proudly to death, trying to show their contempt for

33

the whole business. The thing is, some curse you with a look, some with words and more than once I've been spat at by prisoners – but in the end, they all curse you, or their gods, or both. And that's what Jesus didn't do.

Angelo He didn't curse you?

Tony No.

Simon He should have done! I would have done!

Tony Maybe, son, maybe – but if Jesus had cursed me, I wouldn't be here now. He didn't curse me, though.

Angelo What did he do?

Tony He asked God to forgive me! Me! The one who was putting him to death! It's that which keeps me here, which brings me here!

Angelo Hadn't you heard him speak? Hadn't you heard him teach?

Tony Be reasonable, pal. If I'd turned up at one of his meetings I would have been about as welcome as a ham sandwich at a bar mitzvah. Anyway, my Aramaic ain't that good, as you can tell. I knew he was a good man, though.

Angelo How?

Tony Once, he healed my Captain's servant – without even coming near him! A Roman – and he healed him! He was no criminal.

Simon So why did you do it? Didn't you think –

Tony I'm in the Legion, son. The Legion doesn't pay me to think. It pays me to do what I'm told. It's what I'm best at.

Simon Killing people!

Tony Following orders . . .

Angelo You must wish things had been different.

Tony The moment I received my orders this morning, I wished things were different. 'Three criminals to be executed by crucifixion,' they said. I never dreamed that one of them would be him, but he *was* one of them, and I had my orders . . . if I hadn't followed them, maybe . . . but there. I can't change the things that have happened today, can I? It's done . . . but he forgave me. And that's changed things.

Angelo Why?

Tony Why? Isn't it blindingly obvious? If he'd spat at me, cursed me, pleaded with me – then it's just another execution, isn't it? One more routine killing on the orders of the Governor: one more corpse to be stared at. From my point of view, just more of the same.

Angelo And now?

Tony Now it's tomorrow that is changed, even if I can't change yesterday, or what has already happened today. Jesus forgave me – and made me look at why I needed to be forgiven in the first place, and opened my eyes to what's really important – not following orders from other people, but following God. Not blindly following the crowd, going along with things for the sake of a quiet life. Gave me a clean slate, even while he was in agony . . . so he really *was* him, then.

Angelo What do you mean, 'him'?

Tony Him. *Him.* The Son of God.

This section concludes with an original song. It was commissioned by a Methodist church in the Medway Towns (now closed) which wanted a song which could be performed by two singers with a guitar on Easter Sunday. Since the church was called St Peter's, and Peter played such a pivotal role in the Easter event, it seemed appropriate to write a song reflecting Peter's relationship with Christ and in particular his running to the tomb in the early morning of Easter.

The music is easy for a moderate guitarist to play, either in strum or finger-pick style and is simple enough for two singers to harmonise. I didn't write the music, so I can say with no false modesty that this deceptively simple tune is one of those which stays in your mind all day once you've heard it, and you find yourself humming it while doing the washing-up or walking the dog – so be warned!

YOU RAN TO HIM

You said, 'I love you, Lord',
Put your life in his hands,
You gave it all you had,
But then you slipped away
Like the shifting sands.
You said, 'I love you, Lord',
And ran straight for the shore,
But you cried out for his touch,
Then your faith disappeared
And you wavered once more.

You took so long to understand
Why he died for you,
Why soldiers pierced his hands
and his side for you,
But you ran to him,
Though inside you still wept,
Yes, you ran to him,
While Jerusalem slept,
Yes, you ran to him.

You said, 'I love you, Lord',
And gave strength to the lame,
And though a simple man,
You filled the Church with grace
And our rock became.

You took so long to understand
Why he died for you,
Why soldiers pierced his hands
and his side for you,
But you ran to him,
Though inside you still wept,
Yes, you ran to him,
While Jerusalem slept,
Yes, you ran to him.

Set to original music by Simon Tatnall

You Ran to Him

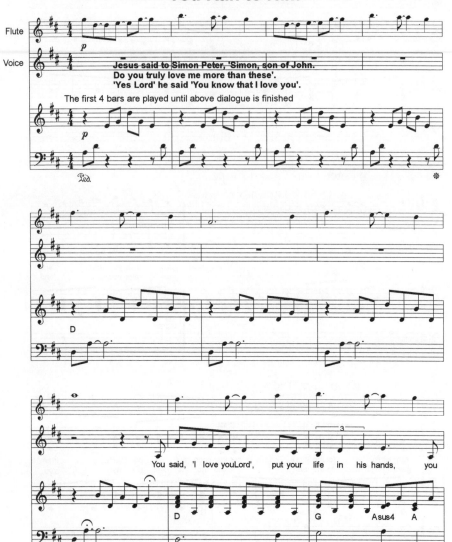

Flute

Voice

The first 4 bars are played until above dialogue is finished

You said, 'I love you Lord', put your life in his hands, you

gave it all___ you had, and then you slipped a-way___ like the shift-

D   Em   Asus4   A

ing sands.   you said, 'I love you Lord', and
                                              said, 'I love you Lord' and

D   D
                                              legato

ran straight___ for the shore, but you cried out for his touch, then
gavestrength___ to the lame and tho a sim-ple man you

G   Asus4   A   D

your faith dis - a - ppeared   and you   wav-ered once more._____   You
filled the church with grace   and your   rock be-came._____

Em   Asus4   A   D

took   so long to un-derstand_____   why He died   for you,   why

D   G   Asus4   A   D/A

sold - iers pierced His hands   and His   side   for you,   but you

D   G   Asus4   A

40

ran to him,_____ though in - side you still wept, yes, you

D   D7   G/B   Asus4   A

ran to him,_____ while Jer - ru - sa - lem slept, yes, you ran

D   D7   G/B   Asus4   A   F#m

to_____ him.

1st time

you

A   A7   D

41

OBSERVERS

A series of monologues for the Sundays in Advent

The Easter series –BYSTANDERS– seemed to work well in preparation for Easter, so it was a natural extension of the technique to apply it to Advent, the time of preparation for Christmas. As this series was written for the same congregation, they were familiar with the format.

Rather than invent characters, however, this series takes characters who are named in the Bible, but rarely figure to any great extent beyond one or two brief incidents. It might surprise you, as it did me, that Andrew, for example, although named with relative frequency in the gospels, is very rarely in the forefront of events, so he has a legitimate and honoured place in this series.

Needless to say, most (if not all) of what follows is fiction, because there are no further records of most of the people featured here – even Andrew disappears into obscurity early on in the Acts of the Apostles!

Each of the characters lights one of the Advent candles. Usually in Advent, as week succeeds week, each leader would light one, two, three, four or five candles. For the purpose of the drama, though, in this series, the previous weeks' candles are lit already before the piece is presented, so that each performer only lights one candle, no matter in which week their piece is performed.

EUTYCHUS

I have to say that it gets rather boring to be called 'the boy who fell out of the window' all the time – especially when you are sixty-three. Don't people think I have done anything else with my life, for heaven's sake?

I have been married for over thirty years, I've got lads of my own and even my lads have got lads. I'm a merchant, I've built up a trade in leather and I'm a Roman citizen – and in Troas they *still* call me 'the window boy'!

I suppose it's understandable, in a way. After all, I *did* fall out of that window, when I was just a young lad. If *you* had had to listen to Paul, going on and on in that hot room and just waiting for him to finish, you would probably have fallen asleep, too. Granted, you might have had more sense than to have fallen asleep on the edge of a twenty-foot drop, but I bet you would have nodded off.

The strange thing is, it seems like I've spent my life waiting, and not just for the preacher to finish. When I first felt the touch of the Spirit, when I was baptised, I thought that we would all be sent out, messengers for God, for Jesus, but nothing seemed to happen in that regard and I used to get so frustrated when I was young. I was so desperate to *do* something for the faith. I would work in the tannery for my father during the day, and at night I would come home to find mysterious strangers sharing the evening meal. Most of them would just be passing through and we'd never see them again. I can't even remember most of their faces, let alone their names: but they would all be on the way to *somewhere*, they'd all been entrusted with some mission, some task, some *purpose*.

My parents would put them up, and feed them, and send them on their way again and listen to their news and hold letters for them or from them – and I would go through the daily round, just waiting. Waiting for the call. Waiting for my turn, my turn to *do* something.

Oh, I know the Messiah has come – you don't have to give me lessons in theology . . . and I don't expect Jesus to appear in front of me, covered in the glory of heaven, or anything, the way Paul described it as happening to him, but it has taken me a long time to realise that I'm not a Paul, or a Barnabas, or a Luke. I'm Eutychus.

I'm Eutychus, the leather merchant – the boy who fell from the window and who seemed dead and who Paul revived by the grace of God, and who spent a lot of his time waiting for the call, before he realised that he had been answering it all along.

You see, I never went on a mission, in the end. As far as I know, God has never used me to convert anybody. I picked up the business when my father died and expanded it, and became prosperous. I married – the daughter of one of the prominent members of our fellowship – and had sons (as a man should) and watched them grow.

And all through the years, Syntache, my wife, and I have fed the travellers, and put them up, and held their letters, and listened to their news, and collected money from the believers to aid the mission – just like our parents did. And all the time I waited – waited for the call.

Do you know, I was sixty before the sign came. I was sharing a meal with my wife and two sons and an evangelist who was passing through Troas at the time. He was just a young man – Marcus was his name – and he'd been travelling for some weeks. He was on his way from Rome to Antioch, which had a large Christian population at the time. He'd just retold us a story his father had told him. It was about the call of the first disciples and Marcus' father had heard it straight from Simon Peter himself. When he finished, I sighed. Syntache said, 'Eutychus, that's a beautiful story – why are you sighing?'

So I told her: how I wish I had heard that sort of call myself; how I longed to follow Jesus and be like Peter and the other disciples and be *doing* something for my faith. When I finished, Marcus burst out laughing, so – rather crossly, I suppose – I asked him what was so funny.

'Why, Eutychus – you've been following Jesus for years!'

I didn't know what he meant, so I asked him. He said, 'Every evangelist and apostle who has ever passed even vaguely near Troas has been fed at this table. In every fellowship from here to Rome and probably on to Jerusalem, everyone who has ever travelled to spread the Word knows where to come for shelter, haven, peace and safety, on the road. We couldn't do it without you and Syntache! We could never have done it without you – you've been following Jesus all along!'

What he said made me feel a lot better. There's still a bit of me that wishes I could have gone out on the road for a while in Jesus' name, but at least I've been a staging post. So I'm lighting this candle for everyone who waits in hope for the promise of God. I know that sooner or later he'll fulfil that promise.

PRISCILLA

We first met Paul in Corinth. I was there with my husband Aquila. It had been a terrible time for us. As Jews, we had been expelled from Rome by the Emperor; as Christians, we were treated with suspicion by the Jews in Corinth; and as Romans, with Roman accents and Roman customs, we were sneered at by the Greeks. So Paul, who was almost as much of an outsider in Corinth as we were, was – well, to be honest, he was at the very least quite a welcome distraction.

Aquila and I had set up in business in Corinth – Aquila was a tentmaker – and because Paul and he had the same trade, as well as the same faith, it made sense to team up. Paul's heart wasn't really in it, though. As far as he was concerned, it was a means to an end. It was a way of keeping body and soul together while he spread the word about Jesus.

Mind you, it was wonderful to see the pair of them sitting cross-legged on the floor, a needle in one hand and a length of cloth in the other, talking away nineteen to the dozen about the faith, and the Holy Spirit, and the Scriptures. Although Paul was eager to hear all about Rome and the Christian fellowships there, when it came to matters of faith it was Paul who did most of the talking, of course. I used to wonder how Aquila got a word in edgeways and then I realised how he did it. He would wait until Paul stuck a needle between his teeth to pick up the canvas – and then he would make his point! I once saw Paul nearly swallow his needle in his eagerness to answer a point Aquila made!

Of course, being men, they were completely hopeless at organising themselves, because they were so focused on the Mission (Paul always said it so you could hear the capital letter in that word 'Mission'). So it was left to me to do the business end of the business – getting orders, finding the canvas, and the thread, and the twine, and the tools of the trade. In the end, it was me who made all the travel arrangements, too. Good job I did. If it had been left to Aquila, we would still have been in Rome when the Emperor's deadline ran out.

Paul was very good company. He was like quicksilver. He laughed a lot and made us laugh, too, though you wouldn't believe it sometimes if you read some of his letters. He could lose his temper easily, as well, but that would quickly blow over like a summer squall. The big thing about him, though, was his *energy*. He was so full of fizz that he left you breathless, and filled you with confidence, and almost energised *you*. I'm sure that if it hadn't been for his teachings about Jesus and his prayers with us and for us, we would never have had the courage to go with him to Ephesus, and beyond, when he felt the call.

But the really remarkable thing about this talkative man was his ability to listen. He would listen to a person's words, but he would answer the questions of their hearts and strip away all the trivial things, all the dead things that held a person back, as easily as you or I would strip the bark from a tree, until you could see the answer to the question you were *really* asking. That's why people loved him – and why some hated him.

He could do that because he listened to God. He listened to God even more intensely than he listened to others, and because he listened, God guided him and gave him the right words, and blessed him with the courage to speak those words, too.

Paul used to talk about the Prophets a lot. I never came across a rabbi with as much knowledge of the Scriptures as Paul. He would quote Isaiah, and Jeremiah, and Amos, and Hosea – and of course, Moses. He loved the Scriptures, because they all pointed to Jesus, you see.

He never realised, though, that in his way he was a prophet himself. He spoke God's word about Jesus, crucified and risen, wherever God sent him to speak and to encourage, and to argue, and to listen.

It was because he listened to the Spirit of God and he did God's will in proclaiming Jesus, crucified and risen, that we didn't know quite what to expect from one day to the next. Although we often stayed months or even years in the same place, you could wake up one morning and he would be up and packing the few things we took with us. 'Come on,' he would say, 'we're off. God's calling us to Ephesus.'

It could just as easily be Beoria, or Macedonia, or Jerusalem, or Rome – he was almost capricious, because he listened to God's call and was open to the promptings of God's Spirit. So that's why I think in his own way he was a prophet. He certainly died like one. He must have known that when he went to Rome he was likely to lose his life. He made plans to visit Hibernia, but I think in his heart of hearts he knew he wouldn't get there. Each day was an adventure for Paul, but he knew also that each day might bring with it his death – but he still followed God's call, wherever it led him.

And that's why I'm lighting this candle – to remember God's prophets, who are open to God's promptings and ready to do and to speak his will, no matter what the cost.

ANDREW

I'm not one to push myself forward. My brother Simon calls me 'The quiet apostle', which is hardly fair and not necessarily accurate, but then what else would you expect from Simon? He's the impulsive one – leaps to conclusions, leaps to judgements . . . Jesus called him 'Cephas' and Simon didn't appreciate the irony, even if the rest of us did! Someone once said that it should have been me who was called 'the rock', since I made about as much noise. That wasn't fair either. I could speak when I needed to.

People who knew me thought it was strange when I took to following John, when I became his disciple, but for me John was a revelation. I'd never seen anyone with such a burning love for the Scriptures. I'd never seen anyone who shone so much with love of God. People used to say that he was on fire with the anger of God, but I always say that he was on fire with God's love. If he – John, I mean – if he seemed angry, it was more at the collective blindness of Israel and its spiritual rulers, rather than with individuals. With ordinary people, in one-to-one situations, it was John's wisdom and humanity and – I know you aren't going to believe it, but it's true – his *humour* that came across. He could be a very charming man. Very charismatic . . . but put him in front of a crowd and he often seemed lofty and stern: sometimes almost dismissive.

John never sought popularity. Some said he actually deliberately set out to provoke the elders of Israel, the kings, and the Romans, or that he was setting himself up to be the leader of a new Israel, laying the foundations of a revolution.

None of that was true. John stood up for the truth and for a purity of response to God and God's demand, and he recognised that to respond to that demand was going to be costly, because it demanded two things from him – that he should speak out though it put him at risk, and that he should give way.

He put himself at risk, because he knew that what he said about purity, about righteousness, was not going to go down well with the rich and powerful who were flouting God's law and only interested in maintaining the status quo. John's words made him dangerous to those with the power to silence him, but he knew the risks.

We, his disciples, could sense John's power. There were some of us who used to deride the Sadducees who ran the Temple hierarchy. I remember one day, when John had run rings round a whole group of them who had come out from Jerusalem to debate with him, one of our companions – Joachim, it was – said they were all like a bunch of bleating sheep – stupid!

We laughed, but John went very solemn, then looked at Joachim and said, 'Never underestimate the power of stupid people in large groups.'

He also knew that some others wanted to use him to stir up revolution, to proclaim *him* the Messiah. It would have been simple for John to acquiesce, but he didn't. That was what made John such a great man, rather than a ranting demagogue. He knew he was just a forerunner and that when the Messiah truly came, he would have to give way: and that's what he did. When Jesus came to John and listened to him preach, John felt his power – and gave way.

Two of us were standing, talking to John, when Jesus walked past. John stopped in mid-sentence, watched Jesus and then turned to us and said, '*There* is the Lamb of God!'

We looked and saw Jesus, and instinctively we began to follow him. My companion never looked back, but after a few paces I turned back towards John, uncertain, and hesitated.

John never said a word. He just smiled.

There were many emotions in that smile. There was a certain amount of pride, I think – though whether in Jesus, his cousin, or me, his disciple, I don't know. There was a little sadness, too . . . after all, he had spent a lot of time in teaching me and many others the things of God.

Most of all, though, I think that smile betrayed satisfaction – satisfied that he had played his part and prepared the way, and now it was time to hand over to Jesus. John shooed me off with a gesture of his hands, like a mother sending her children off to play, and so I turned and caught up with Jesus: and I never saw John again.

So I'm lighting this candle for my friend John, the Baptist, who stood up and spoke out for truth, whatever it cost him personally. In some people's eyes the truth John proclaimed diminished him, because he gave way to the greater light of Jesus: for me, though, his humility was the true measure of his greatness.

MARY, THE WIFE OF CLOPAS

People always wondered why Mary and I – Jesus' mother Mary, that is – were such good friends, since we were so very different in character... different in most ways, really. 'Chalk and cheese', they called us. That's nonsense, in my view, and I didn't hesitate to share my view with anyone who had the cheek to say it in my hearing – even though I've been called worse.

Jesus called us the lioness and the lamb, which was much more complimentary and had the virtue of being almost scriptural. To be quite frank, anyone else who gave me any backchat would pretty soon feel the rough edge of my tongue, but Jesus could have called me virtually anything and I wouldn't have minded – I was content just to be there, with him, with his mother, on the fringes. That was how I got to know about the early years and the first part of Jesus' life – on the fringes.

Sometimes, you see, we wouldn't be with Jesus at all, all day. We'd be on the road, ahead of Jesus, with one or two of the disciples for protection and company, looking out for somewhere to stay that night. Mary would talk quite a lot then. But fairly often, Mary and I would just sit on the edge of those vast crowds – on the fringes. We'd watch him teach them, answer their questions – even reach out and heal them. Sometimes we would be so far away that we could barely hear him speak, what with the breeze in our ears, and the chattering of the crowds, and the coughing of the sick, and the endless questions – so we had plenty of time to talk ourselves.

Jesus would deal with them all so patiently – and in that patience, I saw the mirror image of his mother. Oh yes, I know, we talk about Jesus as the Son of God, and so he is – but do we ever talk about the fact that he had a mother, too? How do you think it must have been for her, when she saw her son fulfilling all that had been prophesied about him? Not just the scriptural prophecies . . . but also those which she had heard addressed to her . . . how do you think it must have felt, to know that a sword still waited to pierce her heart because of him? It must have been agony for her – but she bore it with all the patience she possessed.

I have a son too, you know. I am a mother. I *know* about joy and fierce pride and pain. I *know* what it is like to fret over, despair over and even to shed tears over my son. So don't tell me about meek and mild Mary, all right?

Every time we watched him teach, or preach, I could see Mary's face. I could see that great trust she had in God shining out and although I did not recognise it at the time, I saw the pain as well – because she could not protect him from what was to come: but mostly, it was the trust, you know. Mostly, it was the trust, with maybe a smidgin of pride, but you can forgive her that, surely? Every mother here would.

I'd known her for years, ever since she was a girl in Nazareth – she was about five or six years younger than me – and I'd watched her after she'd come back to our town with Joseph, her husband. The boy Jesus would have been about five or six by then and she had another couple of little ones too.

We shared our hopes for our children and our worries. Ordinary worries, God be thanked! It was only when we took to the road with our boys that I learned the true depth of what she had already been through . . . and she kept to herself the worst bit . . . she just plugged away, supporting him in every way she could . . . and knowing all the time that she couldn't protect him. Dreading, I'm sure, what she could only imagine but couldn't comprehend, but nonetheless keeping faith with her promise to the angel, pledging herself to be the Lord's handmaiden.

I loved my friend Mary as much as I loved her son. I stood with her when the Roman scum put him to death . . . it was the only time I ever cried in public. I remember sobbing and saying to her through my tears, 'How can you bear it, Mary? Oh, how can you bear it?'

She was crying too, but eventually she spoke. Her voice trembled, but she said, 'God promises to wipe away all tears, Mary. I bore the pain of his birth – I can bear the pain of his death, too, if I must . . .'

So, because we have the promise of God to wipe away every tear and turn sorrow into joy, and because she never let me or her son down, I'm lighting this candle for Mary and for every woman who bears the burden of motherhood, even though sometimes it tears the heart out.

RACHEL AND JOEL

Joel Everyone else was cursing the Romans, with their stupid ideas for counting all the people. The political hotheads wanted to cause a rebellion over it! Can you imagine that! 'Course not! But then again, can you imagine the greatest power the world has ever seen making such a fuss over counting a few people? In years to come, it will never happen, you mark my words. Still, the Romans wanted to count everybody – and while the hotheads moaned, the rest of us just got on with it. I wasn't complaining. I was doing a roaring trade.

Rachel *You* were doing a roaring trade? I seem to remember that it was *me* doing all the work. *You* were hanging over the bar schmoozing all the new customers!

Joel Well, if I hadn't have been, no one would have heard the knock on the door in all that bustle! Good job I was there.

Rachel It was Joseph.

Joel Well, of *course* it was Joseph. It wasn't going to be the angel Gabriel, was it? There he was, leaning against the doorpost – and right behind him, squatting on the ground, was Mary. More census visitors. He told me who they were and that they needed a place to stay for the night. I asked him straight out – 'Haven't you got any relatives to stay with?'

Rachel You were a bit abrupt with him, weren't you?

Joel Yeah, I suppose so. Mind you, I took to Joseph. He was very direct in his answer. He looked at me and smiled – I think to take the sting out of his words – and said, 'Look, pal, if I had relatives to stay with, do you think I would be knocking on the door of this fleapit at midnight?'

Rachel But you *did* offer him the stable.

Joel	I didn't have any option. Joseph explained the state Mary was in – that she was just about to have her baby. I could hardly leave her to give birth on the hillside in the middle of the night, could I? We gave them the cave where we stabled the animals and I gave them some blankets and a lamp and brought some food and wine out to them when they'd settled. It was only when I handed them over that I realised that Mary wasn't just *about* to have her baby – she was actually in labour. That was when *you* came into it, wasn't it?
Rachel	That's right. Just after you came running across the yard in a panic yelling, 'Rachel, Rachel, she's having it, she's *having* it!'
Joel	I wasn't panicking. I was just . . . concerned.
Rachel	You were being concerned very *loudly*, Joel!
Joel	It was a good job you were there to look after her. All I had to do was get Joseph out of your way. I got to know a bit about him and Mary while we were waiting.
Rachel	I got to know a *lot* about both of them. Mary was amazing. Apart from my own children (all grown up now, thank goodness!) I've attended more births in this town than I would care to count – but I have to say that she was different. It wasn't that she didn't have pains, or that the birth was easy. I don't think any first birthing is ever easy. It was the calm way she went about it. She was exhausted after her journey and lying on a pile of hay, and she radiated peace, and calm, and trust – all through the birth. In-between the labour pains, she told me some of their story: to be honest, I didn't really follow all her talk about angels, and messages, and dreams. Then the baby was born and it was like . . . it was like . . . it was as if we didn't need the oil lamps in the stable. We were just bathed in light.
Joel	Maybe the angels turned up after all.
Rachel	Well, maybe. The shepherds certainly did. They made such a fuss when they arrived – I had to tell them to be quiet or they'd wake the baby! It was them babbling about 'thousands of angels' which made me understand what Mary had been saying.

Joel	I thought they'd been on the fermented ewe's milk again . . . until I saw the baby. There's a part of me which says it's nice to have had a son to take over the inn from me, but I'm not a great one for babies: all new-born babies look like King Herod to me . . . but this baby was different.
Rachel	You mean, he didn't look like King Herod?
Joel	You know it wasn't just that. All babies are special: they're all signs of God's favour, aren't they? But *this* baby was more like a sign of . . . oh, I don't know.
Rachel	Fulfilment?
Joel	That's it! Fulfilment! And . . . hope. As if God was making some kind of statement to us all though *this* child.
Rachel	And to think, he made that statement in our stable.
Joel	Yeah. I'm glad I'd cleaned it out that day!
Rachel	Are we going to light the candle, then?
Joel	Yeah. Let's light it for the baby Jesus.
Rachel	And the birth of hope in the world.

This is a song which was written in response to an invitation to submit original songs for a new children's songbook for the Christmas season. In fact, the publisher's specific brief was not to mention any of the traditional elements of the Christmas story: the challenge was to insert Christian-based morality into what was overtly a non-religious song.

I think I succeeded – but the publisher turned down my effort anyway. Perhaps in this affluent society, too much mention of the conspicuous poverty which marks the lives of four-fifths of the world's people would spoil the enjoyment of the remaining fifth.

The tune is a traditional English folk tune, which is very simple to learn.

CHRISTMAS CONTRAST

Before you open Christmas cards,
You guess what scenes they'll show –
There's holly, robins, Christmas cake,
And tons of pure white snow.
You never see a Christmas card
In any shop or store
Which shows the desperation of
The hungry and the poor.

The advertising tells us all
That we can find true joy
In the latest innovation, or
In this year's favourite toy:
And still we are unsatisfied
And still we reach for more,
But ignore the situation of
The hungry and the poor.

We'll stuff ourselves to bursting, and
Pretend it isn't greed;
We'll give each other presents that
We'll never, ever, need:
And then, when Christmas passes, and
It's back to work once more,
We'll deplore the deprivation of
The hungry and the poor.

Sung to the English folk tune 'Edwin'

Christmas Contrast

Smoothly - pedal for every 2 beats

(verse lines)

Be - / The / We'll

fore you op - en Christ-mas cards, you guess what scenes they'll show There's
ad - ver tis - ing tells us all that we can find true joy. In the
stuff our- selves to burst-ing, and pre - tend it is' - nt greed; We'll

holl- y, __ ro - bins, Christ-mas cake, and tons of pure __ white snow you
lat- est __ in - o - va - tion, or in this year's fav' - rite toy: And
give each __ o - ther pre-sents that we'll ne - ver, e - ver, need: And

ne - ver see __ a Christ-mas card __ in a - ny shop __ or store Which
still we are __ un - sat - is - fied __ and still we reach __ for more, But ig -
then, when Christ - mas pass - es, and __ it's back to work __ once more, We'll de -

TRANSFIGURATION

There are two Sundays of the year which you can guarantee will cause most preachers to groan. One of those is Trinity Sunday – for obvious reasons – and the other is the Transfiguration. Many preachers either steer clear of this subject altogether, because it is so difficult to explain, or they attach explanations to it which, if examined, they have obviously, in the words of my children, 'made up out of their own heads' and which would horrify the professional theologians and Bible scholars amongst us.

This monologue makes no attempt to explain the reasons for the Transfiguration – it merely tries to illuminate its effect on those who witnessed it. It was performed at three Anglican churches in Co. Kildare, Ireland, on the Feast of the Transfiguration in 2001, and was well received.

Having always lived amongst the fishermen on the lakeside kind of prepared me for being amongst the disciples. The fishermen were rough and ready men, hard as nails, and weatherbeaten, and as ready with a kind word as they were with a cuff on the ear for the young lads among them. Apart from the cuffed ears, of course, because Jesus never liked any kind of violence, the disciples weren't much different. My mother always used to say that if you put any group of men together for any length of time, you always ended up with a bunch of rowdies. I remember she said once that God made Eve so that he didn't have to spend all his time keeping an eye on Adam. My father snorted and said, 'Well, it's a pity God didn't make someone to keep an eye on Eve, then, bearing in mind her track record!'

Mind you, the similarities stopped there. We didn't go with Jesus just for a kind of extended 'lads night out'. He was teaching us: I don't know about the others, but for the first time in my life, all the things we'd learned from our village rabbi began to make sense. That may seem strange now, now that folk are talking about us Christians as if we had sprung from nowhere. You might expect me to say that everything Jesus taught us was new. In a way it was, but only because it cast a different light on what we already thought we knew. I don't think I ever heard Jesus say anything which he couldn't relate to Torah in some way: it was just that he made it so real, and relevant – and accessible.

My family has never been one for all the Temple ritual, quite frankly. We think of ourselves as good, observing Jews, but seeing all those priests parading around in their finery in that huge Temple when we go down to Jerusalem for Passover doesn't impress us at all. All those pious Pharisees, with their prissy squeamishness and their holier-than-thou attitudes put us off religion, and that huge Temple, although it is impressive, always gives me the feeling that being close to God is beyond the reach of the poor and the ordinary. I mean, how could you live like that, if you've got a living to make? How could you hope to be holy if you were ordinary people like Andrew and Simon, and James –and me? But Jesus changed all that.

You see, although he was like us – same accent, same rough and patched clothes, the same easy, free stride as he walked along the dusty roads – he was also unlike us. There were moments when he was speaking to us when I could have sworn . . . well, the only way I could possibly describe it would be to say that it was almost as if he was speaking to us from a long way away – as if he was speaking to us from somewhere else, somewhere else entirely. He would tell a story about sheep, or harvest time, or something and then he would say, really quietly, 'The Kingdom of Heaven is among you', or something like that, and it would send shivers up your spine . . .

He would make you realise that it was possible to be ordinary, and yet to do God's will, to act and live in the way God intended us to. In a funny sort of way, it was because he was so ordinary that he was so extraordinary. Then, one day, something happened which showed that extraordinariness. I'm not talking about . . . you know . . . what happened in Jerusalem that last Passover time . . . it was before that.

He was in the habit of taking one or two of us off with him sometimes and leaving the others to fend for themselves for a while. It wasn't always the same ones, although usually either Simon Peter or Andrew would be among them. This time, the time I'm talking about, it was Simon Peter and James, and me. Before dawn, Jesus woke us and told us to follow him. In the pitch black of the night, we walked up this high mountain: don't ask me which one, they all look the same to me. I thought we were going up the mountain to pray. Jesus liked to pray at dawn in a high place. When we got near the top, my brother and I turned round to watch the dawn come to the valley, but Simon kept his eyes on Jesus, who was pressing on to the summit.

I noticed some wild goats further down the slope and I was going to point them out to Simon. Just as I turned to him, he looked over my shoulder, his eyes widened and his mouth dropped open. James and I turned round to see what caused his reaction: and then our eyes bulged too. We must have looked a real sight, three grown men with their jaws on the floor.

Jesus stood there on the summit of the mountain, and, well . . . shone. He wasn't just bathed in the light of the rising sun. It was as if the sun had risen within him, rather than around him. His face, his hands, his feet – it was as if they were bursting with light. Even the clothes he was wearing seemed to catch some of that glory, because they were so dazzlingly white that it was almost unbearable to look at them.

The three of us fell to our knees, struck dumb, almost battered to our feet by the power of what we saw. Then, just as we began to get used to it, the air around Jesus changed . . . the only way to describe it is to say that the air *thickened*. I know that sounds stupid, and it all seemed to happen in the blink of an eye, but that's what it looked like. The air kind of *shrank*, all of a sudden and then . . . oh, it's no good, I'm no good with words . . . Look, you know what water looks like in a pot, when you are boiling it? You know how that still surface suddenly erupts with a huge bubble and steam bursts from the surface of the water? Well, it was as if the air around Jesus did that, and all the time he was ablaze with light and out of the disturbance in the air, like air bursting from boiling water, two men appeared, looking just as bright as Jesus and then . . . they just talked with him.

I couldn't hear what they were saying, but I knew who they were. It's no good asking me how I knew they were Moses and Elijah, I just *did*, OK? I mean, who else could they be? Anyway, Simon had obviously thought the same as me. He tried to speak.

James and I just knelt there, hoping the blazing light wasn't going to consume us. To be fair to Simon, at least he tried. I could hear him clearing his throat desperately. If the inside of his mouth had dried from fear as quickly as mine had, then I'm surprised he could speak at all. Mind you, it was typical of Simon, because when he did speak he said something really stupid, something about building booths, one for each of them. That's how I knew he had recognised Moses and Elijah too. He named them.

None of them bothered to reply and before Simon could repeat what he'd said, the air around us changed. All of a sudden, we were in the middle of a cloud – it just kind of appeared. If was as bright as day, but we couldn't see through it . . . and then we heard the voice.

I knew it was the voice of God, because it was like no other voice I've ever heard: it seemed to penetrate my entire body. Just the sound of it was enough to throw us face down on the floor. I really thought I was going to die . . . the voice said, 'This is my beloved son – listen to him!'

Eventually, and it seemed like ages but was probably only a minute or so, I looked up – and Jesus was alone and smiling down on the three of us, cowering on the ground. No Moses, no Elijah, no cloud – and no voice. Jesus looked as he always had – rough clothes, sunburnt face, tangled beard. 'Get up, boys, get up!' he said, 'We've got work to do – down there!' and he pointed down into the valley.

On the way down, he told us not to tell the others what had happened – not until everything was accomplished, he said. We were too stunned to ask why, but we never did tell the others. We never even spoke about it amongst ourselves for years: but every now and again, when Jesus did some miracle of healing, or when his words changed the way people thought, I would catch Simon or James' eye and we would smile at each other, and we would remember.

We would remember the sun rising within him: and it would rise for us, too.

Wonderful as our various hymn and song books might be, I have found that the Transfiguration – probably for reasons of the theological obscurity referred to above – has been neglected. Unless you want to sing 'Stay, Master, stay upon this heavenly hill' every time (not that there is anything wrong with that venerable old favourite) there isn't much of direct relevance to the Transfiguration to offer congregations in the hymn department.

This hymn is an attempt to offer something for churches to sing on this Sunday, but it need not be confined to this Sunday. It is set to a well-known tune which has already been used for at least two hymns in *Hymns & Psalms*, so the congregation need not be distracted from the words by needing to concentrate on a new tune. For the musical historians amongst us, the words were written on a coach travelling through southern Germany in July 1999, when the writer was accompanying a party of elderly people from a German

Methodist Church on a day trip to a former Imperial Castle in Baden-Wurttemburg!

O LORD OF ALL THE EARTH

O Lord of all the earth,
We come to hear your word and sing your praises;
Your love has brought to birth
The hope which Jesus now within us raises:

O come to us, we pray,
In Word and song and story,
Inspire us all today
So we proclaim your glory, your glory,
Your glory, your glory!

O Lord of time and space
Through Jesus Christ you promise us salvation;
And shining from his face
Your love enlightens every race and nation:

O come to us, we pray,
In Word and song and story,
Inspire us all today
So we proclaim your glory, your glory,
Your glory, your glory!

O Lord of wind and flame,
Who comforts every heart that has been broken:
The stars declare your name,
And deep within our souls your love is spoken:

O come to us, we pray,
In Word and song and story,
Inspire us all today
So we proclaim your glory, your glory
Your glory, your glory!

Sung to the tune 'Vreuchten' – HP 213

A GOOD ENOUGH CHRISTIAN

This piece is designed to be used to start a service. There should be nothing before it (hymns, prayers, whatever). The person playing God (and it can be male or female) ought not to be in view of the congregation. A radio microphone would be useful for the character of God!

George is busying himself, getting the church ready for the worship service

God George!

George *(looking startled)* Who's that?

God It's me, George.

Pause

George There's an awful lot of 'me's' around here. Could you be a little more specific?

God How many 'me's' do *you* know who speak to you out of thin air?

George Not too many, but there used to be times when my mother would –

God Nice try, George, but no cigar. Do I *sound* like your mother?

George Well, no . . . So give me a clue.

God The wholly Other; the Numinous; the Kerygma; the First Cause; the Alpha and Omega; Ground of Being . . . *Me.*

George I asked for a clue, not an entry from Roget's *Thesaurus.* And I *still* don't – oh, God! *(claps hand over mouth)*

God By George, he's got it!

George You don't really mean . . . no, no, this is a joke, right?

God Nope.

George But you can't be . . . well, you know, *Him.* I mean, I was just about to talk to you, man – I mean, God – if you

	are God, that is – I mean I was just getting the church ready for the service so that we could *all* . . . well . . .
God	Listen to the word of the Lord?
George	Well, yeah.
God	So why aren't you listening to me right now?
George	I am. I *do!* It's just that I never really expected to . . . *(tails off)*
God	You didn't expect to actually hear me, right?
George	*(miserably, and feeling awkward)* Right – no, wrong! It's just that I've just got used to the idea of *me* talking to *you.* I never expected you to . . . well, to . . .
God	To talk back to you? Well, it's not exactly my normal method of communication, but there are precedents.
George	Pardon?
God	Sometimes I like to surprise people. Moses, Joseph, Elijah, Isaiah, Paul – people like that.
George	But why me?
God	You've got something in common with all those people.
George	I have?
God	Sure.
George	What's that?
God	I've got a job for you.
George	*(startled) What? (violently shakes head)* Oh no, not me! *(hides on all fours under pulpit)*
God	If I may borrow a phrase from one of my more inspired human creations: George – don't do that! *(pause)* There've been other people who've tried to run away and hide from one of my jobs, George. I'm pretty good at persuading them, though I say it as shouldn't. Remember Jonah? That whale idea was really one out of the top drawer!
George	I'm scared.
God	You haven't heard what the job *is* yet, George.

George	Maybe not, but I've got a pretty good idea.
God	So what do you think it is, then?
George	Listen, if you're God, you know what I'm going to say, so why should I bother saying it?
God	*I* know what you're going to say next, George, but so far in your short life there's pretty good evidence that *you* haven't got a clue – so go on, surprise me.
George	It's going to be something along the lines of 'Go out into the world, preach, heal, baptise' and all that stuff, isn't it?
God	Hey, you *did* listen to my Son, after all – but you left a word out.
George	*(comes out from behind the table)* Which word?
God	*All.* 'Go out into *all* the world . . . ' Not just the bit you feel comfortable in. Not just the people you feel comfortable with. All. Everybody. The works. The whole enchilada. So that's what I want you to do.
George	How can I do that? I'm not the sort you're looking for at all.
God	Why not?
George	I'm too young.
God	By the time he was your age, David had led an army of thousands into battle.
George	You mean he was younger than me when you had this kind of conversation with him?
God	Yep.
George	*(triumphantly)* Then I'm too old!
God	Abraham was no spring chicken when he went on a journey on my behalf – he was seventy-five!
George	*(chastened)* Well, anyway, I don't have the expertise.
God	You're a Christian aren't you?

George	Yeah, but I'm not that sort of Christian. I'm not a *professional* Christian. I haven't got a dog collar – I haven't even got a dog!
God	Every Christian is that sort of Christian – and you don't *need* a dog collar. Or a dog. All you need is to trust me.
George	I'm not a good enough Christian. Can't you send someone else?
God	My Son was talking to everyone when he said he was sending you out like sheep amongst wolves – not just those with the gift of the gab, or the brains of a mainframe computer.
George	I don't know, God. You do seem to choose the most unsuitable people.
God	I choose everybody, George. You're all as suitable as each other.

Pause

George	Sheep amongst wolves, eh?
God	Sheep amongst wolves, George. What d'you say?
George	Baaa!
God	That's my boy!

The Wild Goose Resource Group of the Iona Community have for a number of years written and published collections of two-handed sketches under the title 'Eh, Jesus? Yes, Peter?' which are short, funny and incredibly insightful. They are easy to insert into a service, and relatively easy to perform.

I thought it would be useful to st – to adapt this idea for a Methodist congregation. Since John Wesley travelled extensively in Cornwall (and even had a house there), a fact of which Cornish Methodists seem inordinately proud (it never seems to occur to them that he came so often because there was so much of the work of salvation to do in that county), it seemed appropriate to make Cornwall the destination of his next journey, to remind the Methodist people of their itinerant and evangelical roots, and to remember that there is often a cost associated with discipleship.

HEY JOHN . . . YES, CHARLES?

Charles   Er . . . John?

John   Yes, Charles?

Charles   You know this outdoor preaching thing . . .

John   Yes – what about it?

Charles   They don't like it, you know.

John   Could you be a little more precise about this, Charles? *Who* doesn't like it?

Charles   Well, people.

John   Which people?

Charles   Well, *everybody*.

John   You really mean yourself, don't you?

Charles   *(splutters)* Well, I was never keen, you know, but you can't say it has exactly won you friends, has it?

John   I went down very well in Cornwall.

Charles   If you gloss over the regrettable incident in Falmouth.

John	The people were keen to hear me.
Charles	So keen they put in the window and began to demolish the house . . .
John	Hundreds, nay, thousands were converted in Bristol!
Charles	And they dragged you by your hair to the village pond and tried to drown you in Wednesbury.
John	No they didn't. That was in, oh, let me just cast my mind back . . .
Charles	Well, if it wasn't a drowning in Wednesbury, it was a stoning in Pensford.
John	. . . no, Wednesbury was where they tore my coat and cut my hand.
Charles	Well, whatever it was, you have been in severe danger.
John	Pensford was when they tried to set a mad bull on me!
Charles	See what I mean? Lawlessness, vandalism, lynching, mad cows . . . what century are we supposed to be *in*, for heaven's sake?
John	But it isn't anything to *do* with the century, is it, Charles? You know that. Some people have *always* had a vested interest in maintaining the status quo. Even the mindless mobs are really being egged on by the landowners, the clergy who resent the power of our preaching, those who aren't interested in changing lives for Christ's sake.
Charles	I see that, but, well . . . don't you think that the Lord might be saying, 'That's enough, John – time to move on to something else?'
John	I'm glad you see it my way! Right – on to Truro!
Charles	No, no! You know I don't mean that . . .
John	So what do you mean?
Charles	Well, perhaps a change in lifestyle. Settle down. Get married. Find a nice, quiet little parish somewhere . . .
John	Charles, you know that in the matter of preaching the Word –

Charles	Don't say it –
John	You know quite well that I consider –
Charles	Yes, yes, I know!
John	I consider –
Charles **John**	*(together)* The world is my parish.
Charles	You would be amazed at how often you have said that over the years.
John	I cannot say it often enough. You know the tremendous amount of work there is to do . . .
Charles	Yes, John, but it's all so *different* –
John	Different from what?
Charles	From the Church we were brought up in, which we expected to serve.
John	Which we still serve, Charles, each in our own way. You write hymns –
Charles	Which you seem to feel at liberty to alter!
John	And I travel round exhorting the faithful and encouraging the faithless –
Charles	And inciting the mob!
John	Charles, that was unworthy of you!
Charles	Unworthy, but true. When we first started out, I was as enthusiastic as you. Still am, I suppose – but look at the trouble we've caused.
John	Look at the souls we've saved.
Charles	But it's all so, so . . .
John	Exciting?
Charles	Yes, but it's all so . . .
John	Awe-inspiring?
Charles	*Yes,* but it's also all so *frightening* and *unsettling.*

John   You don't really think that God is going to seize this nation by making it *comfortable* or *sedate*, do you? When the Holy Spirit is at work, making all things new, saying, 'Behold, I do a new thing', you don't really think he means just more of the same, do you?

Charles   Well, if you put it like that . . .

John   Of course you don't! When the rushing wind of the Spirit drives people to do his work, then things are bound to be unsettled, bound to be a little bit scary. In fact, I would be surprised if they weren't . . . hold on a moment. This is pretty well what I was going to say on my next journey.

Charles   Where is it this time? Cornwall again?

John   Yes, I'm off to Liskeard. Quite the pleasantest town in the county. They have large and serious congregations. They like me there. They say I'm just like a proper Cornishman.

Charles   What, alternating between 'inspiring' and 'infuriating'?

John   *You* may say that Charles, but *I* couldn't possibly comment!

On the face of it, this sketch would seem to have little to do with faith in general and Christianity in particular.

However, there are many Christians around whose ignorance of the Bible is astounding – people who often make it up as they go along in the 'The Bible says . . .' game. It's usually a bit of a giveaway that they don't know what they are talking about, because they will often say, 'I'm sure the Bible says somewhere . . .' when they are trying to bolster a spurious argument.

Bible study ought to be as much at the heart of each Christian's walk with God as prayer and worship and social action – but I fear that it is one of the sadly neglected disciplines: and yet we expect Christians to evangelise! I am quite sure that if car mechanics showed the same propensity to parrot something they have read from a book without having first studied the principles behind what they are spouting, then the garage would pretty soon run out of customers: and that's the origin of this sketch . . . I mean, you wouldn't go to a garage mechanic like the ones in the sketch below, would you? So why do we suffer the same breathtaking level of ignorance from our members?

Designed to be used on Bible Sunday in particular, but usable on other occasions, this sketch seeks to illustrate that concept with humour.

THE MECHANICS

Dramatis Personae

Graham Payne	– the junior mechanic
Phil	– the senior mechanic
Mr McLaren	– the customer

Mr McLaren   Ah! There you are Mr Payne! I've been trying to get you on the phone all day! Have you found the cause of our problem?

Graham   Oh! Er . . . hallo, Mr McLaren. Yes. Well . . .

Mr McLaren   I hope it won't take too long to fix?

Graham	(*sucks air through front teeth*) Wouldn't like to say, I'm afraid. You've got a problem with yer diffbox, aincha?
Mr McLaren	Have we? What precisely does that mean?
Graham	Well, yer bearings have gone *in* yer back wheels, which has caused a reciprocal uneven load *on* yer rear axle, thus causing a stripping *of* yer cogs in yer diffbox and therefore a loss of power.
Mr McLaren	Which means what, exactly?

Pause

Graham	Well, it means that, it means that . . . yer bearings have gone *in* yer back wheels, which has caused a reciprocal uneven load *on* yer rear axle, thus causing a stripping *of* yer cogs in yer diffbox and therefore a loss of power.
Mr McLaren	So we can't drive it?
Graham	Er . . . no.
Mr McLaren	Er . . . Mr Payne – have you actually looked at our car?
Graham	Mr McLaren, I have been in this garage since I left school. I know about cars, believe you me.
Mr McLaren	So you know about ours?
Graham	Of course.
Mr McLaren	So you won't need me to tell you that our car is front wheel drive.
Graham	Of course not. I knew that! It's a Vauxhall Vectra.
Mr McLaren	It was a Peugeot 309 when I left here last week.
Graham	Just testing. The 306 –
Mr McLaren	309 –
Graham	*309,* is of course based on the Vectra design.
Mr McLaren	But the 309 was designed before the Vectra!

Graham	*(sneering politely)* I don't think you'll find you'll be right there, squire.
Mr McLaren	Oh yes I am!
Graham	Let's not argue, eh? After all, how much time have you spent in a garage?
Mr McLaren	Not a lot. But enough to know that if a car has front wheel drive, it doesn't even *have* a diffbox to – what did you say it did?
Graham	Er . . . 'ang abaht . . . *(mouths words under his breath until he gets to . . .)* caused a reciprocal uneven load *on* yer rear axle, thus causing a stripping *of* yer cogs in yer diffbox and therefore a loss of power. Yeah. That was it. Definitely . . . unless . . .
Mr McLaren	Mr Payne! Have you actually looked at our car?
Graham	*(waves him away)* 'Ang abaht . . . PHIL!

Phil comes in, wiping his hands on an imaginary cloth.

Phil	Yeah?
Graham	Will you tell Mr McLaren 'ere about 'is diffbox?
Phil	Sure. *(clears his throat)* Yer bearings have gone *in* yer back wheels, which has caused a reciprocal uneven load *on* yer rear axle, thus causing a stripping *of* yer cogs in yer diffbox, and therefore a loss of power.
Mr McLaren	How could that possibly be right?
Phil	*(points at Graham)* Because *he* told me this morning.
Mr McLaren	*My car hasn't got a diffbox!*
Phil	*(to Graham)* You taken it off already, Graham? Quick work!
Mr McLaren	*It's never had a diffbox!*
Phil	*(puzzled)* 'Owdja drive it dahn 'ere then?
Mr McLaren	*It doesn't need a diffbox!*

Phil	*(pleased)* There you go, then – problem solved!
Mr McLaren	*(loudly)* Aaargh!
Graham	Settle down, settle down – I'm sure we can solve this little problem with your Vect – Three-oh-si – nine! 309!
Mr McLaren	Have you actually looked at my 309?
Graham	*(sucks air through front teeth)* Er . . . no.
Mr McLaren	Have you ever worked on a 309?
Graham	*(sucks air through front teeth)* Er . . . no.
Mr McLaren	Do you even have a manual for a 309?
Graham	I think I got one out of the library once, but I had to take it back, it was overdue.
Phil	I've got a manual for your Vauxhall Vectra, though, if that's any use . . .
Mr McLaren	*(loudly)* Aaargh! That's it – I'm taking my business elsewhere! *(storms out)*

Phil and Graham start to move away during the following

Graham	Funny people, customers, ain't they?
Phil	I've known a lot of Vectra owners like that. It's that 'orrible lime green colour they come in. Drives 'em mad.
Graham	That's int'resting. Howdja know that?
Phil	Read it in a book somewhere . . . Peugeot owner's manual, or sunnink . . .

This song speaks for itself – it was written for Harvest Festival, at a church where the harvest gifts consisted of tinned food and tin openers, packed into boxes ready to be distributed in Eastern Europe. It seeks to contrast the 'traditional' view of Harvest which we celebrate with such gusto, rich with images of the pastoral idyll, which vanished long ago, if it existed at all, with the reality of the global village and the desperate conditions of the poor in the developing world.

Since most of our congregation will have grown up in towns, rather than in villages, it might be a little more appropriate than 'We plough the fields and scatter' for the majority of them!

FEED MY SHEEP

At Harvest time we thank our Maker
For the strength that earns our keep:
Can we hear the voice of Jesus,
Telling us to feed his sheep?
Songs are sung of sowing, reaping,
Prayers of thanks for food are said –
But can we hear his children weeping
For the lack of daily bread?

Praise the living God who feeds you,
Praise the Lamb of God who leads you,
Praise the Spirit for his grace,
But don't turn – no, don't turn
Your face from his people.

Jesus fed his hungry people,
Fed them in the Father's name,
Can we hear the voice of Jesus,
Telling us to do the same?
At our Harvest celebrations,
Where we lay our offerings down,
Do we feed the lambs for whom
Our Saviour laid aside his crown?

Praise the living God who feeds you,
Praise the Lamb of God who leads you,
Praise the Spirit for his grace,
But don't turn – no, don't turn
Your face from his people.

Praise the living God who feeds you,
Praise the Lamb of God who leads you
Praise the Spirit for his grace,
But don't turn – no, don't turn
Your face from his people.

Set to original music by Simon Tatnall

79

Feed My Sheep

1. At Har - vest time___ we thank___ our ma - ker for___ the strength___ that earns___ our keep:
2. Je - sus fed___ his hun - gry peo - ple fed___ them in___ the Fa - ther's name.

Can___ we hear___ the voice___ of Je - sus, tell - ing
Can___ we hear___ the voice___ of Je - sus, tell - ing

G   D/F♯   D   C/E   C   D   G

us___ to feed his sheep? Songs___ are sung___ of
us___ to do the same? At our Har - vest

D/F♯   D   C   G   O/D   G/F

sow - ing, reap - ing, pray-ers of thanks___ for food are
ce - le - bra - tions, where___ we lay___ our offer - ings

G/D   D   C   Am7   Dsus4

said but can___ we hear___ his chil - dren weep - ing
down, do___ we feed___ the lambs___ for whom our

D   Em   Bm7   C   D

face from his peo - ple._____ Repeat chorus from 𝄋

A9/C♯   D   G   G   G

♩ = 140

G   C/E   G/D   D   C

Rall

Am7   Dsus4   Dsus4   D/F♯   G

Feed My Sheep

Extra harmony for repeat of chorus

Praise   God   Praise

Praise the liv - ing God who feeds you Praise the Lamb of

God   Praise   God

God who leads you Praise the Spi - rit for his grace but

This is a different kind of meditation, written at the behest of the Women's World Day of Prayer committee of the Parish of Blessington in the Republic of Ireland. They wanted something which reflected the choices people make to lay their lives on the line for a just cause and, particularly, women who lay their lives on the line. They wanted to see the Esther story through the eyes of Mordecai as well as Esther, so they asked me to write something meditative and vaguely poetic, rather than the prose monologues they would otherwise employ: and I had a whole twelve hours to write it in! This was therefore written at the breakfast table of a B&B in Ireland in 2000. Apparently, it was very much appreciated . . . personally, I would have appreciated more notice, because I am sure I would then have changed it – polished it up a little. Nevertheless, it has its own hurried integrity, and therefore 'What I have written, I have written.'

MORDECAI'S CHOICE

Haman rages, spitting death on every Jew
In every far-flung province of the King –
For I, Mordecai, the Jew, chose not to bow,
And would not bend the knee to human pomp.
I could have bowed to Haman, bent the knee:
Perhaps I *should* have, but I chose instead
To stand upon the promise of the Lord,
And risk the wrath of Haman falling on my people's head.
We Jews have always been resourceful folk –
We've made bricks without straw,
Discovered dry pathways across reed seas,
And defeated mighty Midian
With darkness, sunlight, and mirrors.
But what choice did we have?
For we were slaves in Egypt,
Desert refugees caught between the sea
And Pharaoh's chariots: no choice.
Surrounded by our enemies in our own land –
We had to stand and fight: no choice.
And now the choice is mine . . .
If I should choose to try and go before the King,
Although he has not called me to his court,
Then I have made a choice and courted death.
If I should choose to call upon the Queen
And lie in rags and ashes at her gate,
I hand the choice to her, to Xerxes' queen
And place in Esther's hands a people's fate.
So what if I refuse?
Choose not to choose?
Then once more the choice is made,
And death comes calling,
And every Jew in every province dies.
In the face of evil, there is no neutrality,
There is no refuge from the raging storm;
Every action and inaction is a choice.

This hymn was originally written for a nationwide Methodist competition, run in 1988, to find a new hymn, suitable for congregations to sing, to celebrate the anniversary of the conversions of John and Charles Wesley. It didn't win – but we still like it!

CHRIST BE PRAISED

Christ be praised that, fed by faith
There are those who understand
The Father's love must be proclaimed
To all created by his hand:

Praise the Father, by whose power
All creation has been formed;
Praise the Son, whose suffering love
Has redeemed this suffering world;
Praise the Spirit, by whose fire
Christians' hearts are strangely warmed.

Christ be praised, that through the hope
Of saints inspired, we too may spread
The glorious, saving Gospel song –
Jesus lives who once was dead!

Praise the Father ...

Christ be praised that, powered by love,
We may witness to his name;
Yesterday, today, forever,
Jesus Christ is still the same!

Praise the Father ...

Set to original music by Simon Tatnall

Witnesses

♩ = 70

Unison

Christ be praised that, fed by faith
Christ be praised, that through the hope
Christ be praised that, pow'rd by love, of

D   A/D   G/D   A

there are those who un - der stand the
saints in - spired, we too may spread the
we may wit - ness to his name;

D   A/D   G/D   A

fath - er's love must be pro - claimed to
glo - ri - ous, sav - ing gos - pel song that
yes - ter - day, to - day, for ev - er,

D   G/D   D   A

all cre - a - ted by his hand:
Je - sus lives who once was dead!
Je - sus Christ is still the same!

Bm   D/C♯   D   Bm   A

Praise the spi - rit, by whose fire

Christ - ians' hearts are strange - ly warmed.